Hey guys, we're super stoked to introduce the "Lukas Crew" project, a cool initiative all about smashing stereotypes and embracing diversity for kids with disabilities. Created by awesome parents, Antônia and Fabio Yamashita, this project is all about using comic books to teach kids under ten why diversity and inclusion totally rock.

It all started with Lucas, a dude with cerebral palsy, and his parents' determination to make the world a more inclusive place for him and all kids with disabilities. They realized that a lot of prejudice comes from just not knowing enough, so the Lukas Crew is here to fill that knowledge gap with fun and engaging stories.

The main goal? Educate both kids and grown-ups about inclusion and break down the stigma surrounding disabilities. These comic books offer a rad and accessible way for everyone to learn, aiming to shape kids' perceptions and attitudes during their crucial values-forming years.

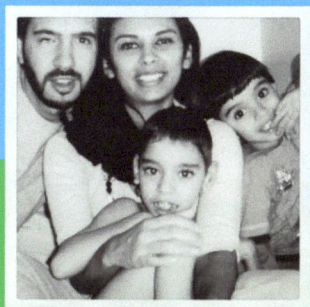

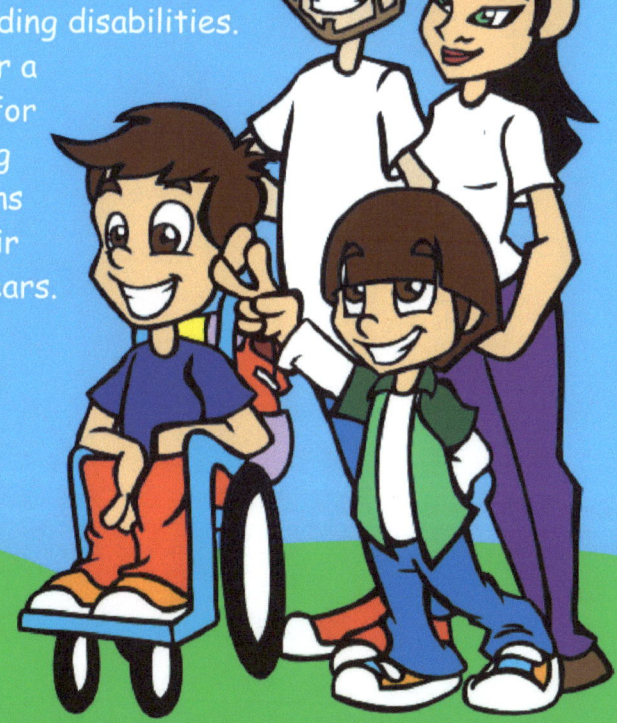

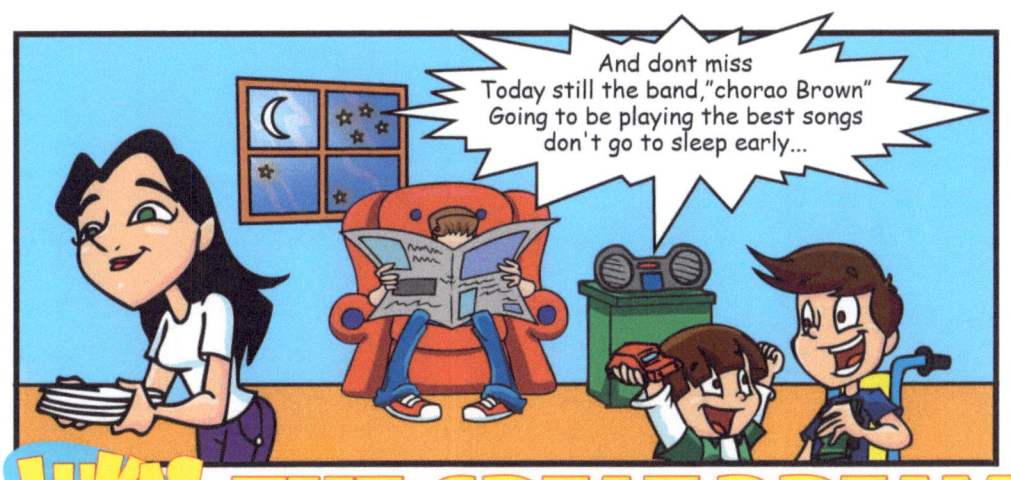

LUKAS GANG: THE GREAT DREAM

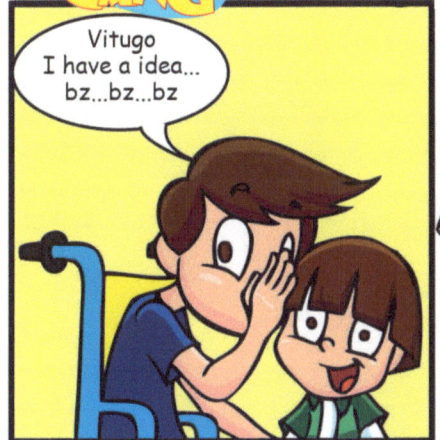
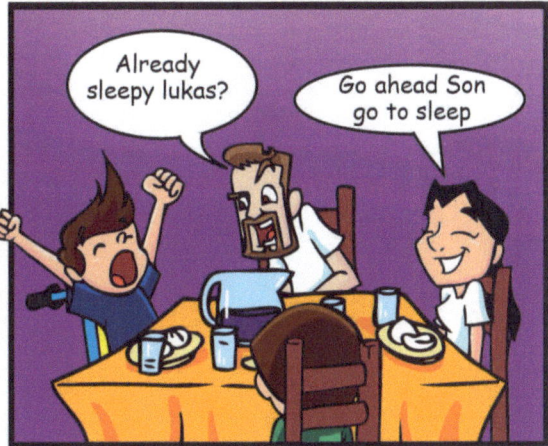
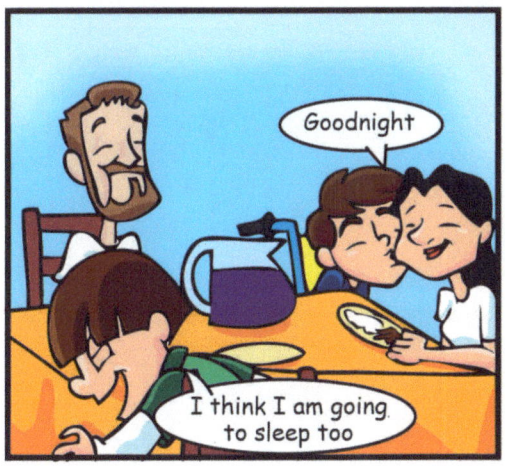
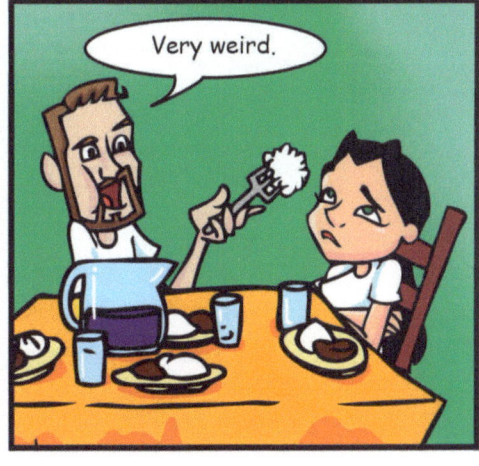

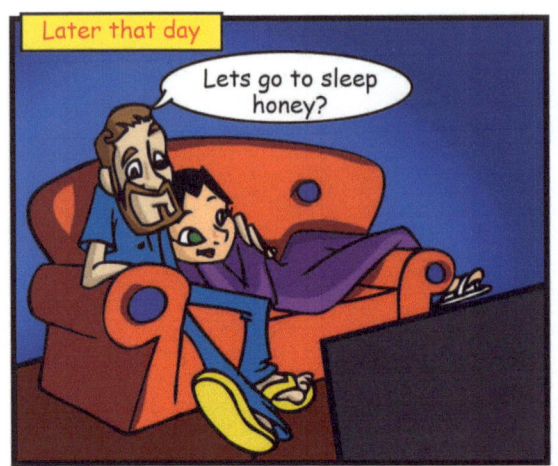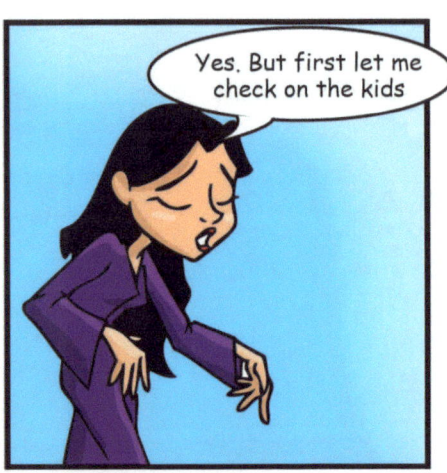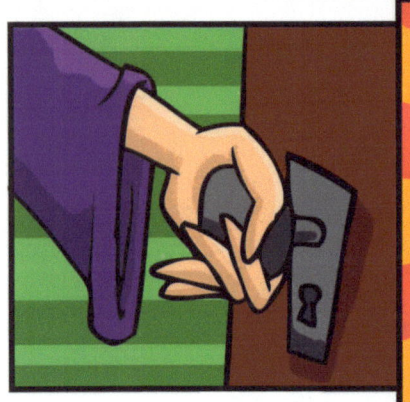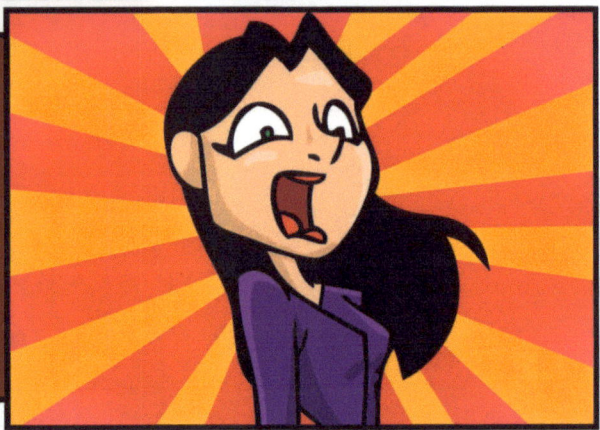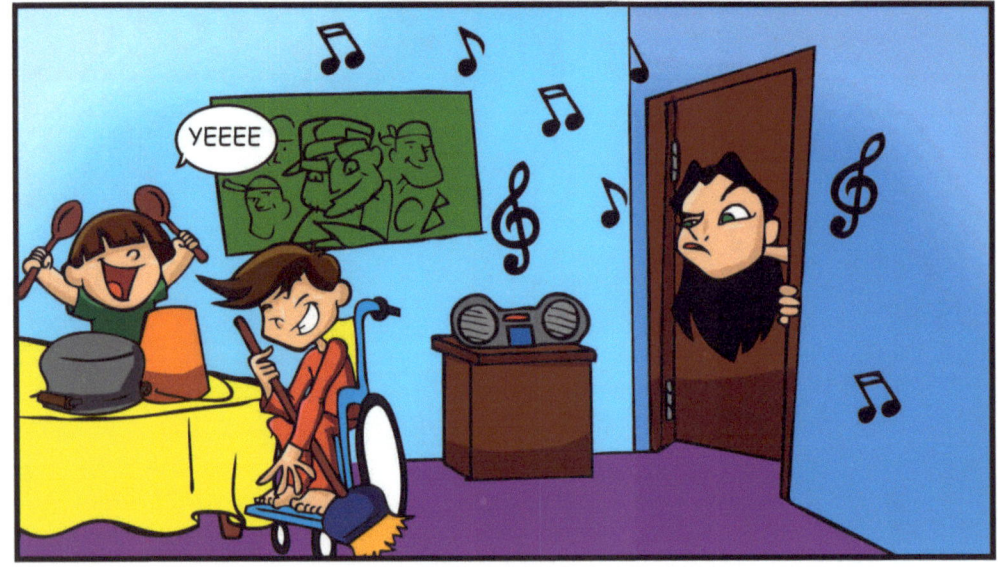

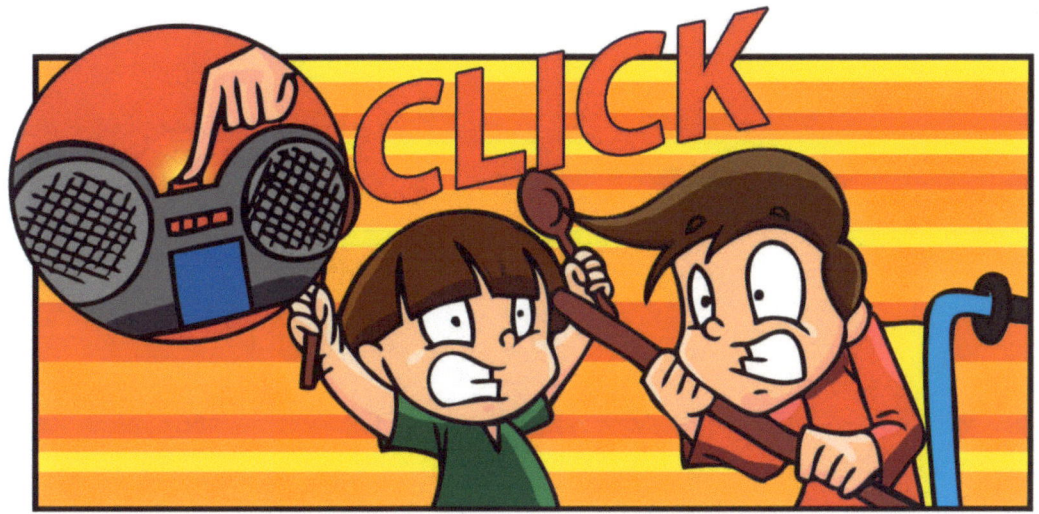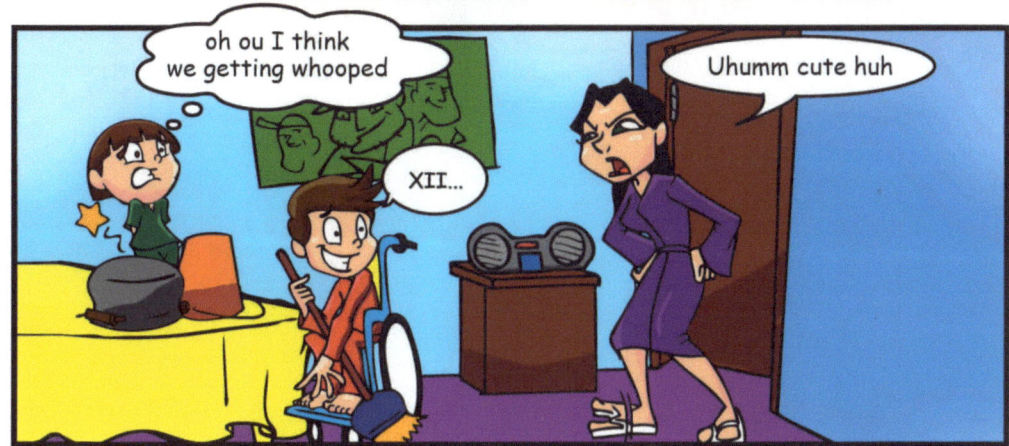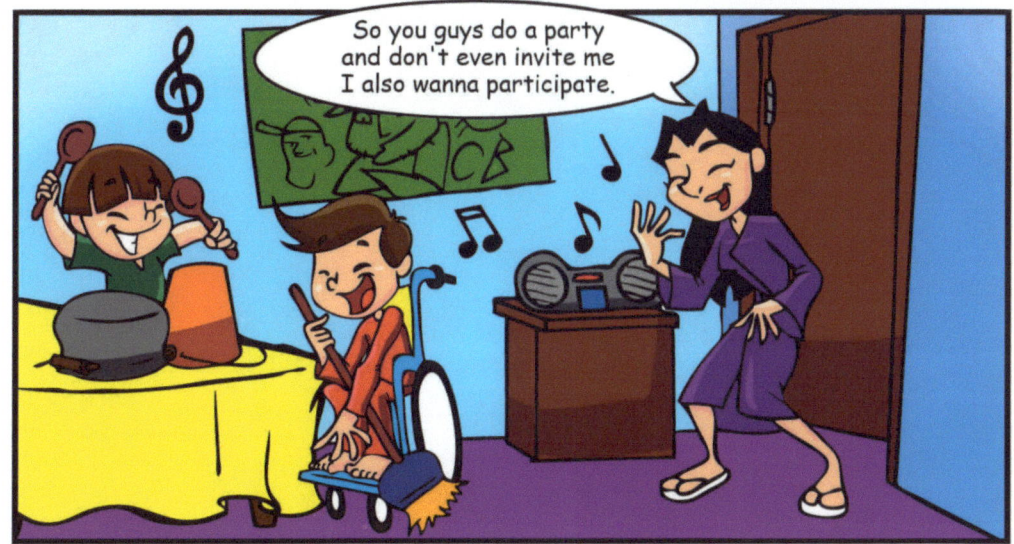

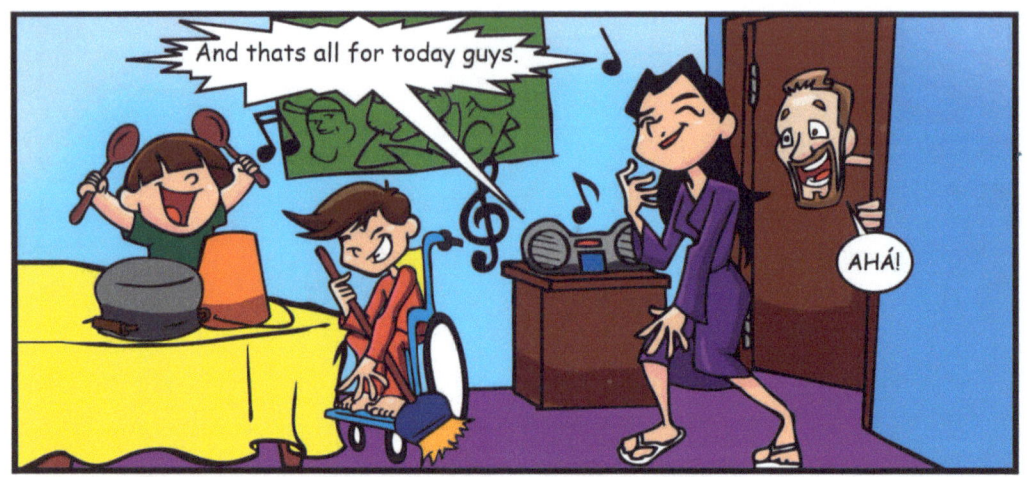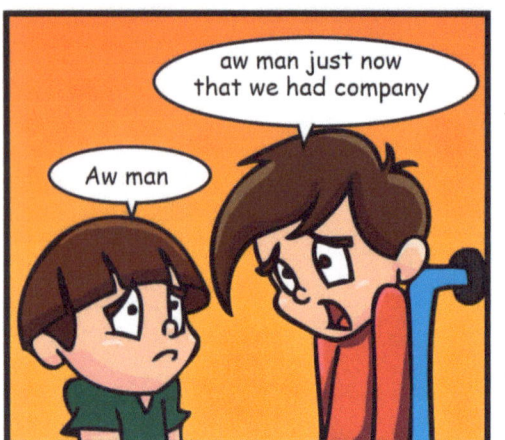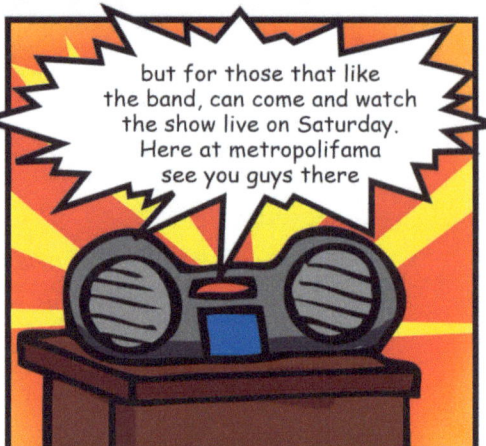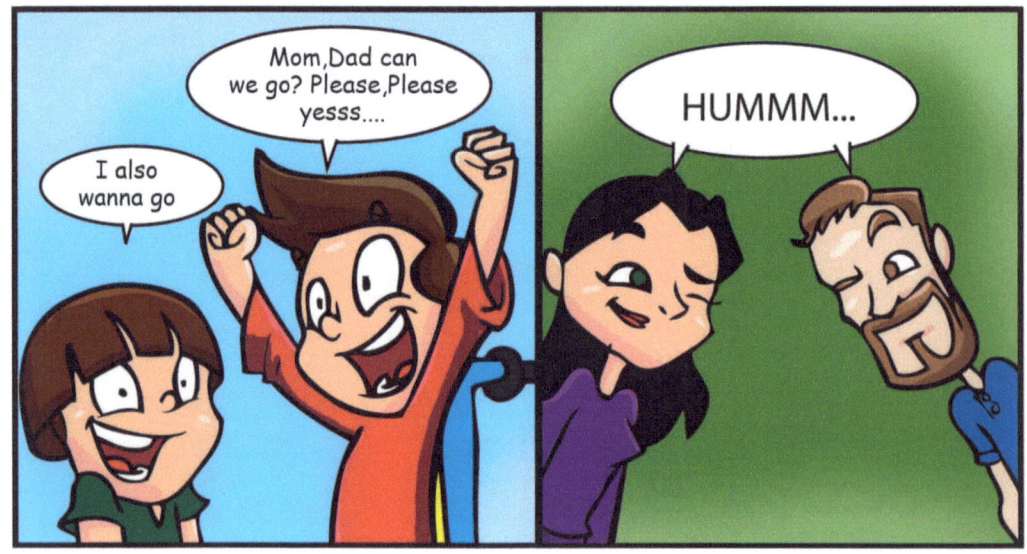

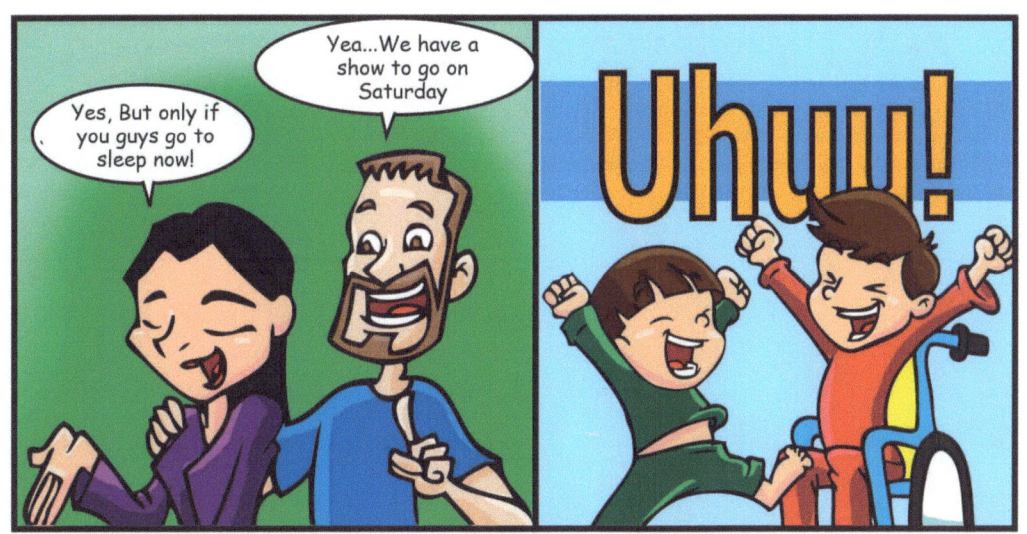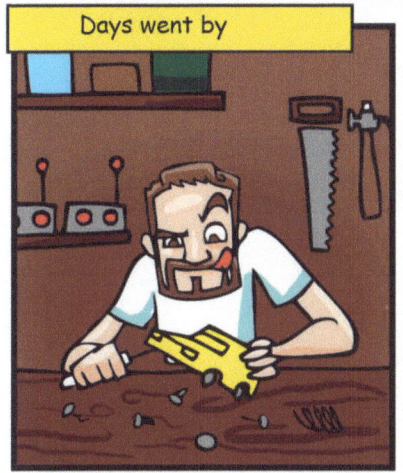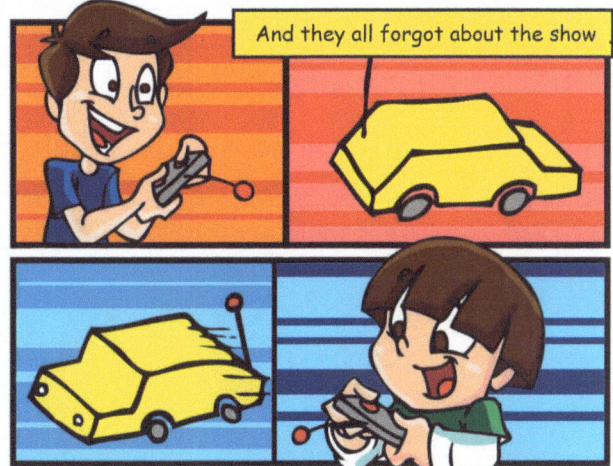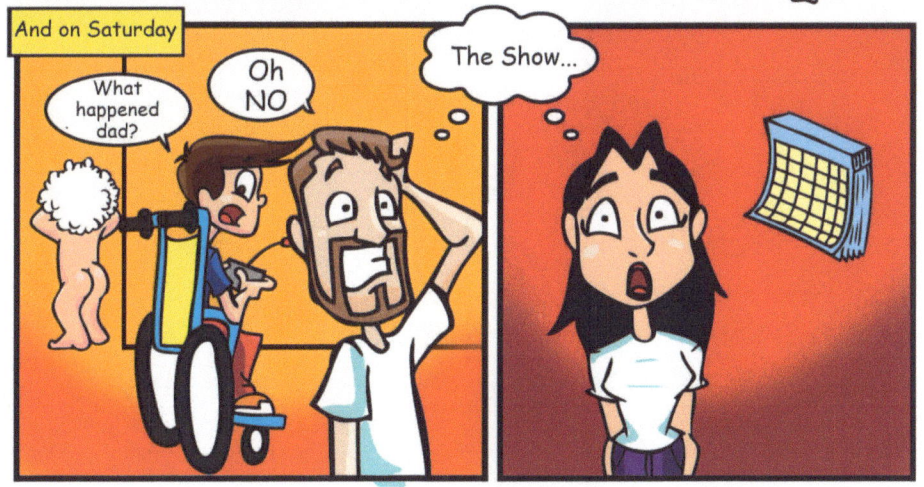

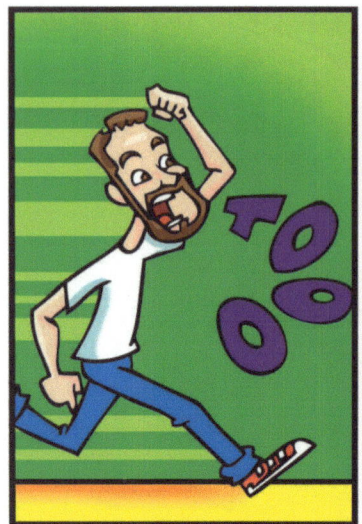
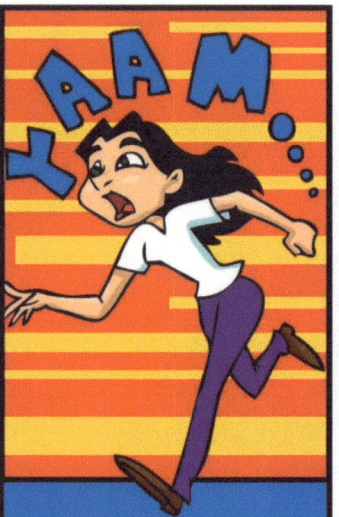
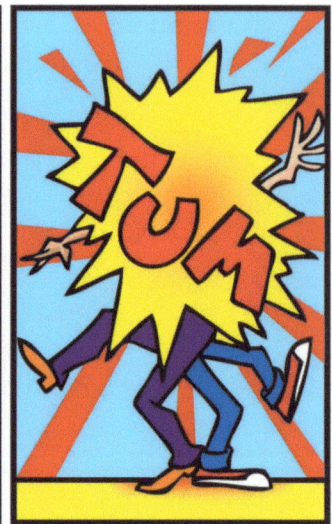
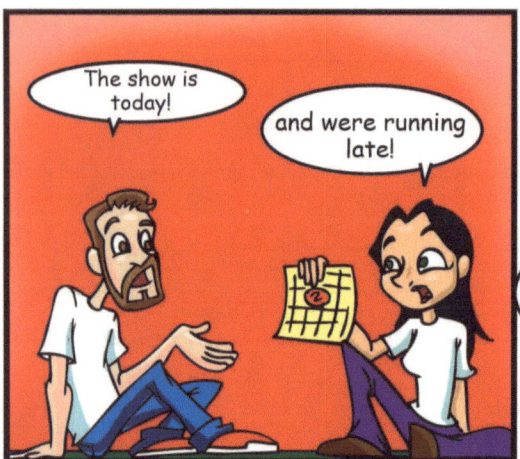
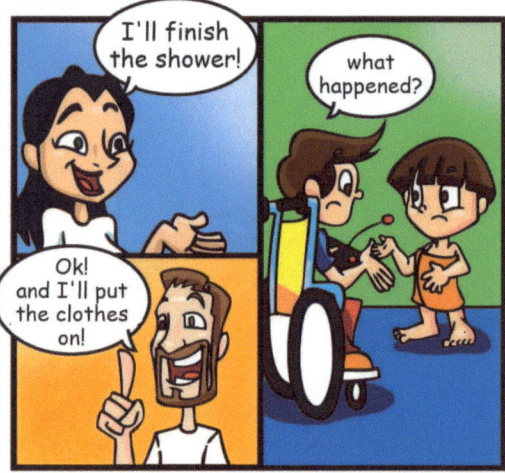
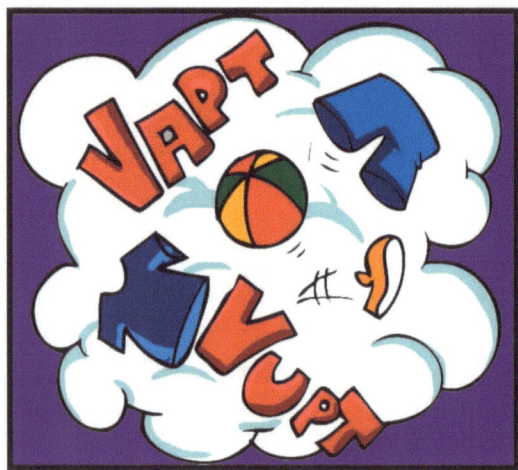
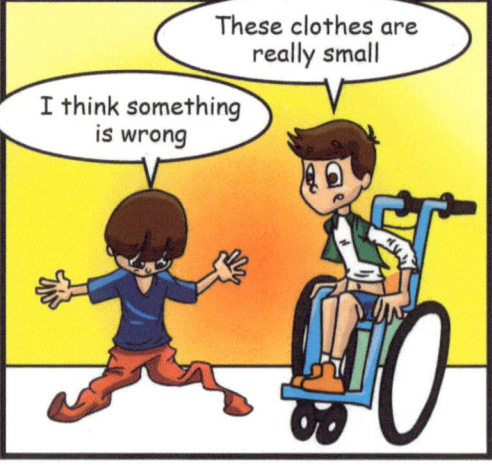

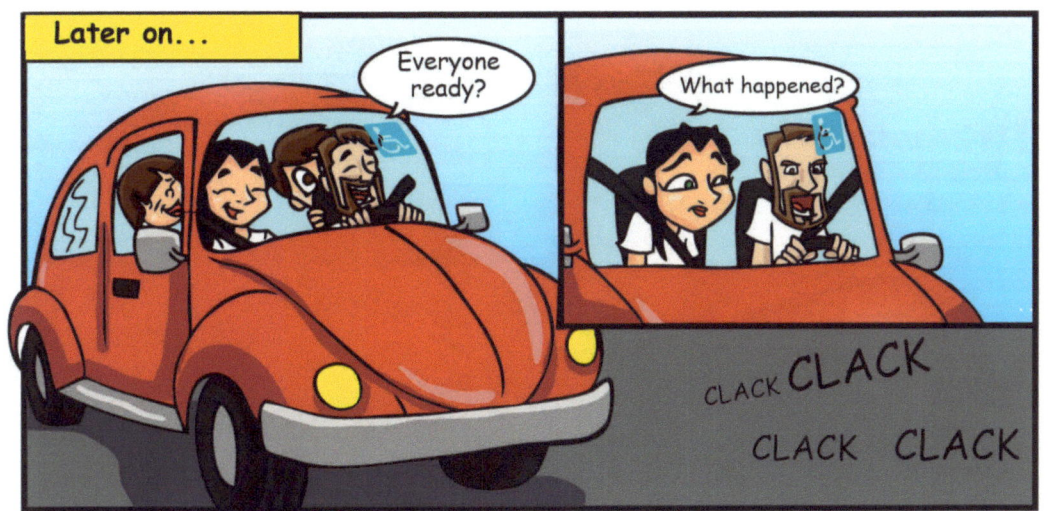
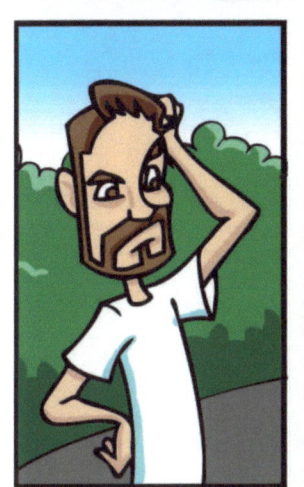
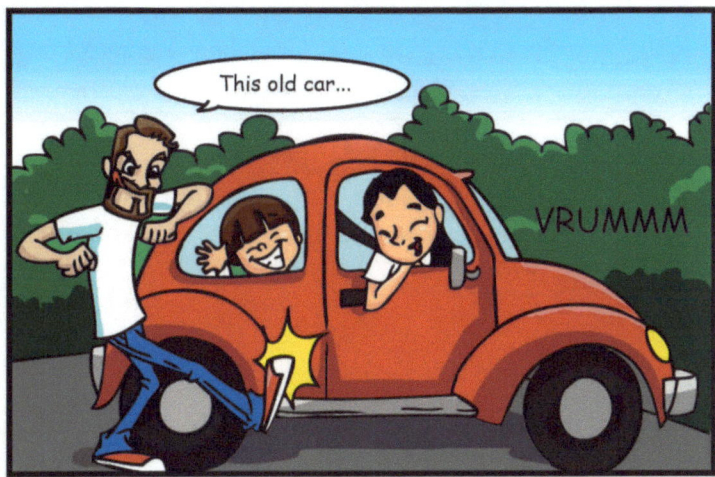
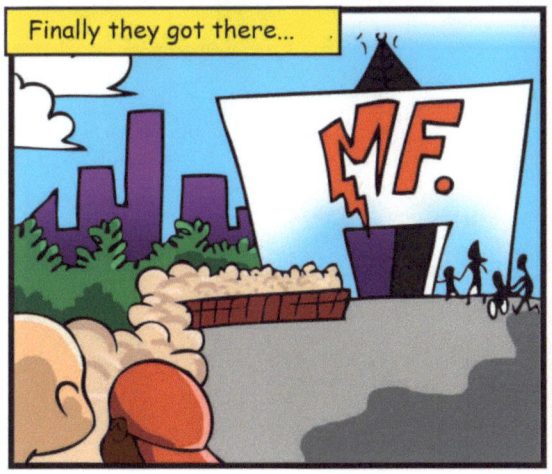
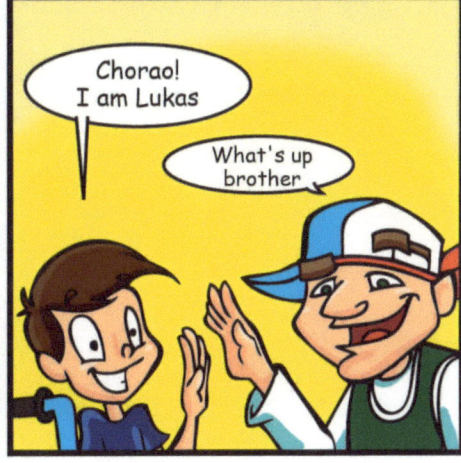

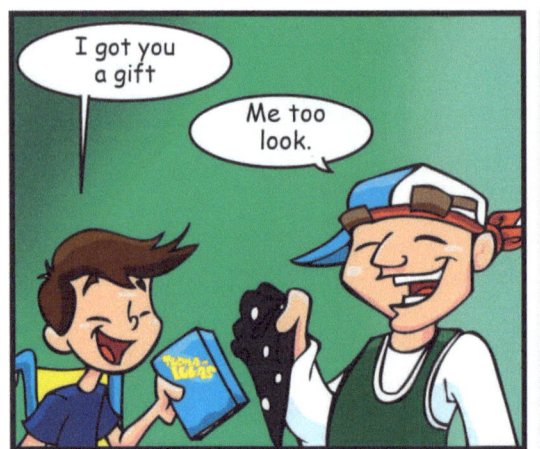
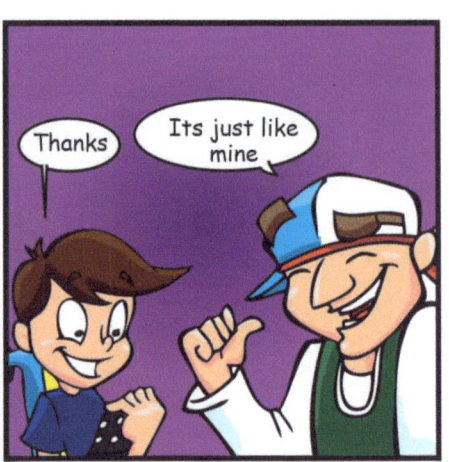
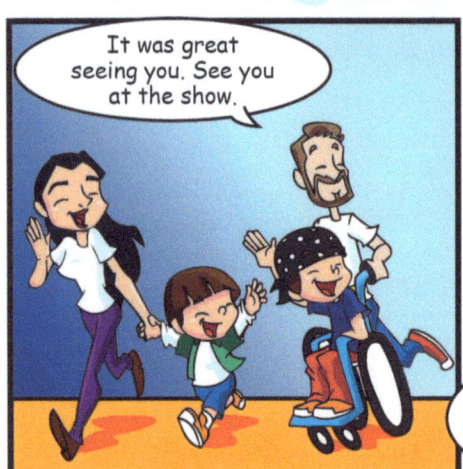
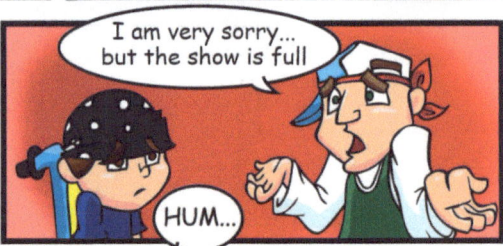
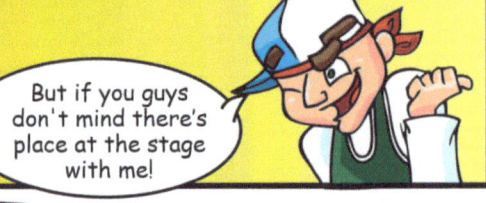
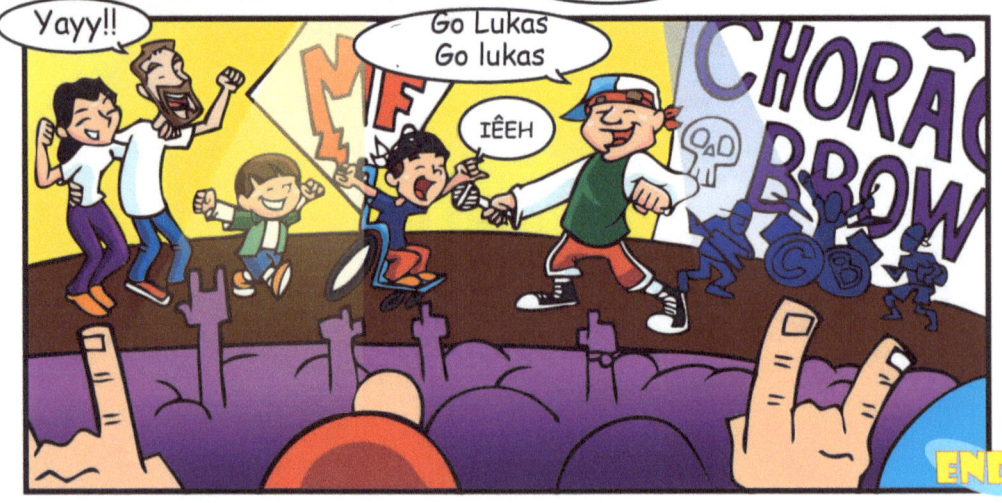

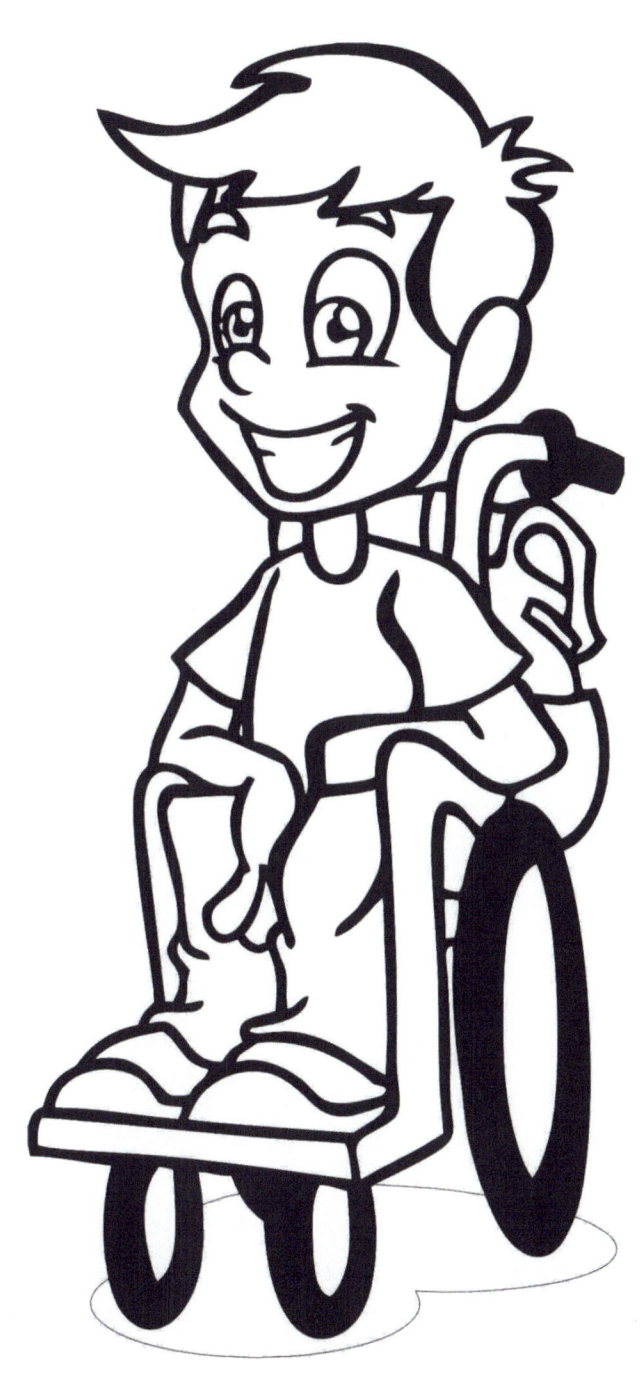

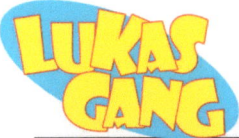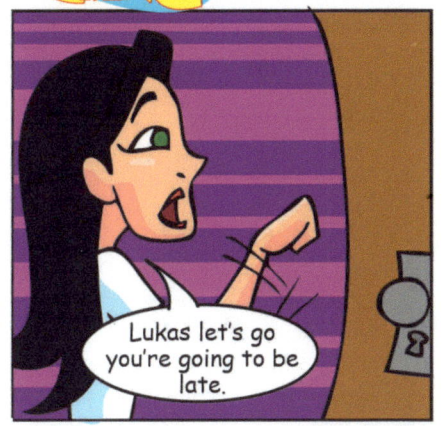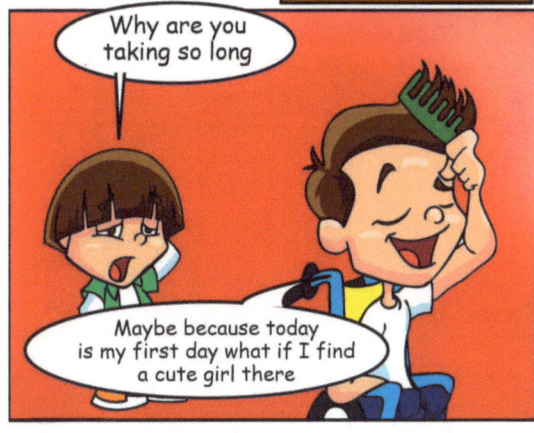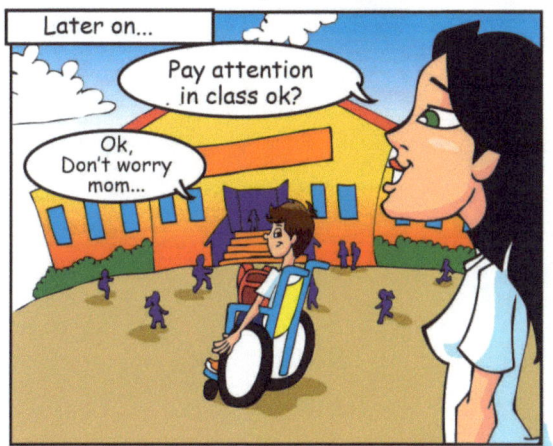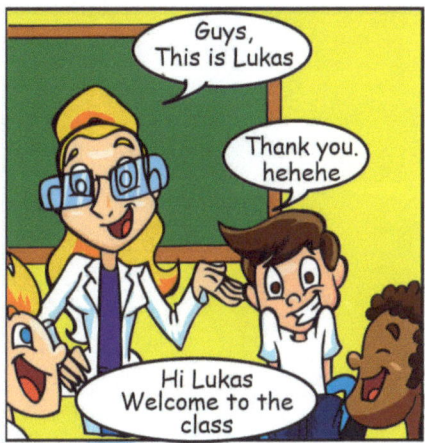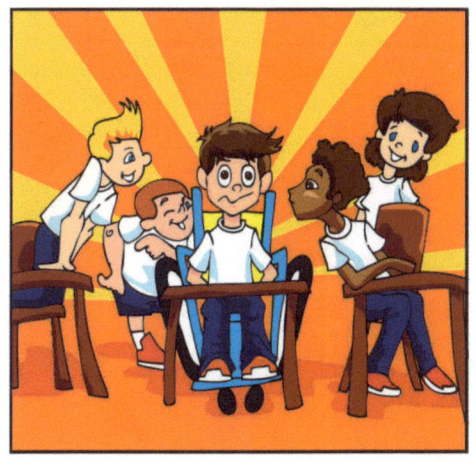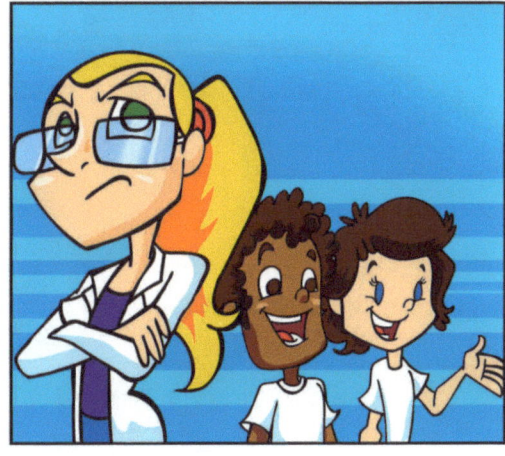

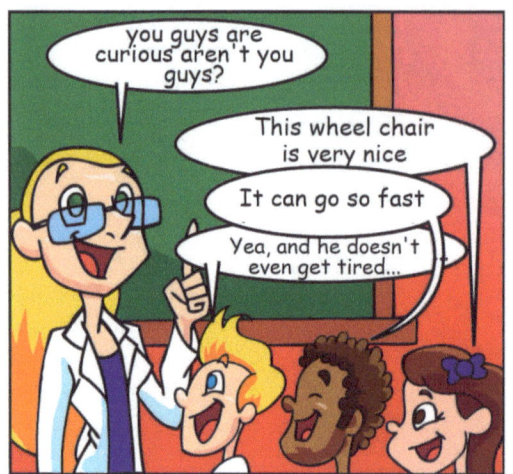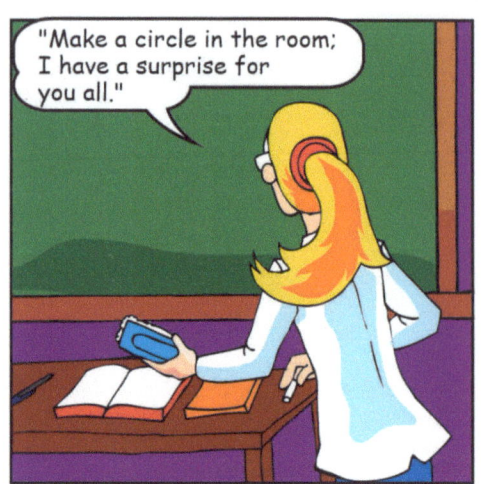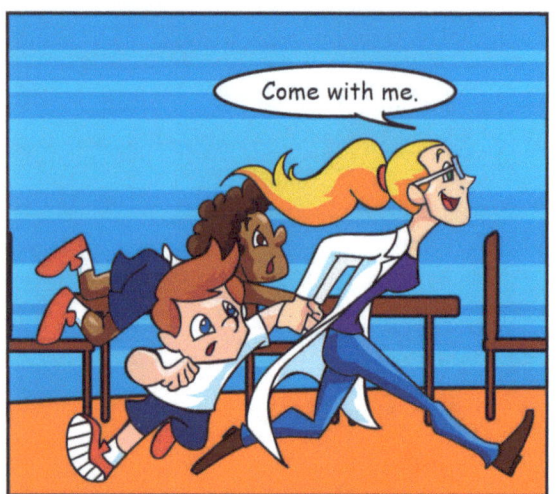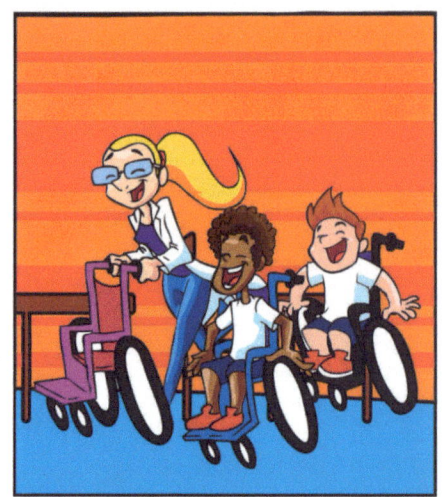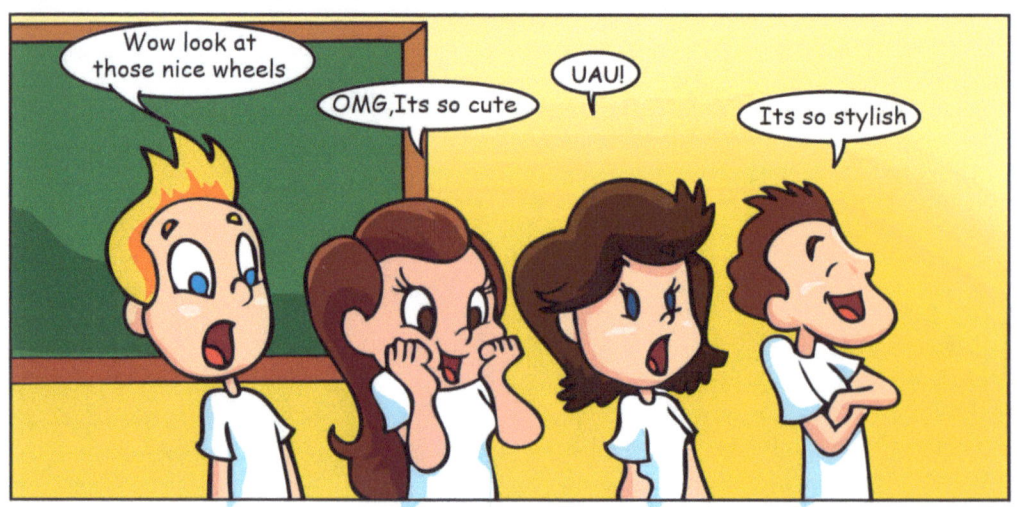

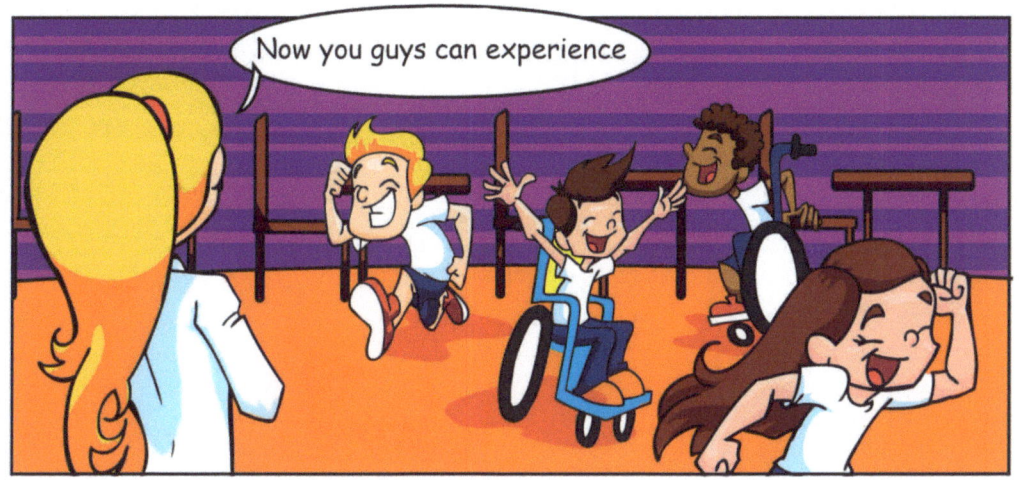
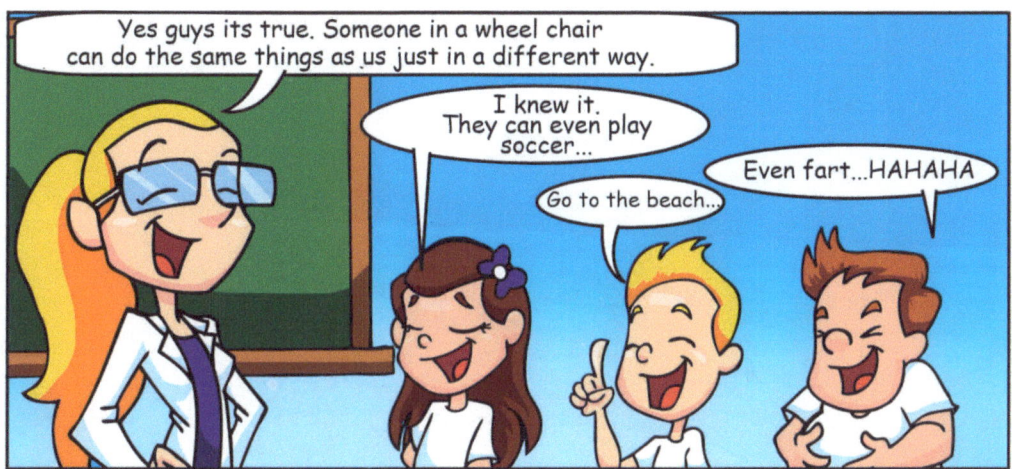
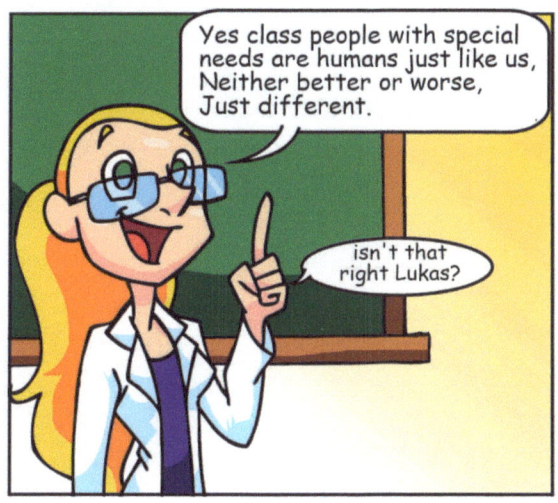
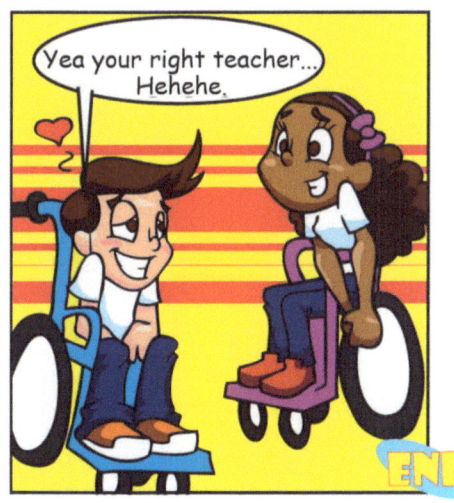

Discover the inspiring journey of Lukas and his family in this heartwarming story of overcoming adversity! From Lukas' birth, battling cerebral palsy, to his first five years of life, his mother Antonia narrates every challenge and triumph with touching honesty. Get ready to be moved and inspired as you dive into the pages of this captivating book.

Witness the unwavering love of Lukas' parents, their tireless determination, and Lukas' own strength of will as they face each obstacle with courage and hope. This story is proof that love and resilience can overcome even life's greatest challenges.

Don't miss the opportunity to get your hands on this touching book on Amazon today. Let yourself be swept away by a story that will touch your heart and leave you with a new perspective on the power of love and perseverance. Purchase now and embark on this unforgettable journey with Lukas and his family!

www.specialneedsmom.us

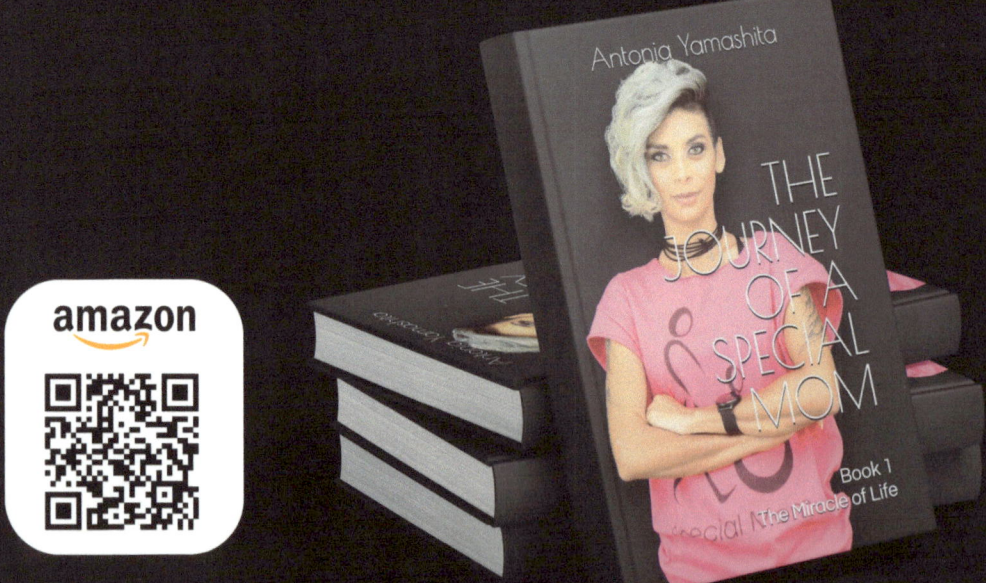

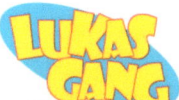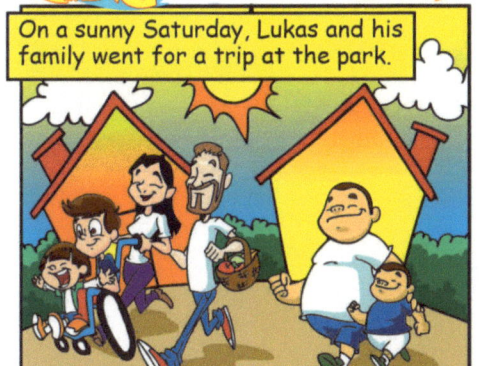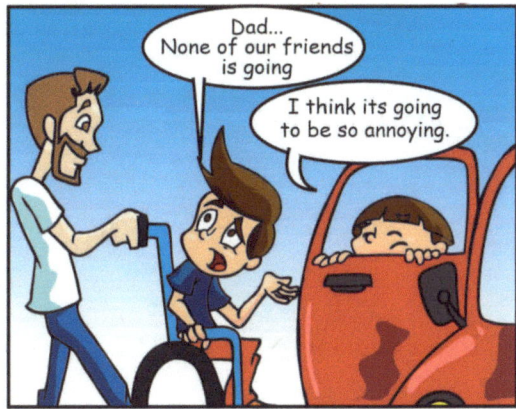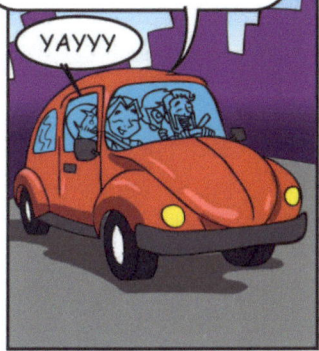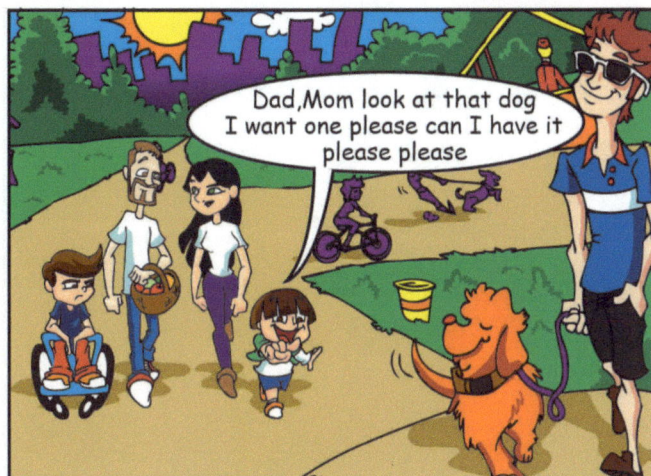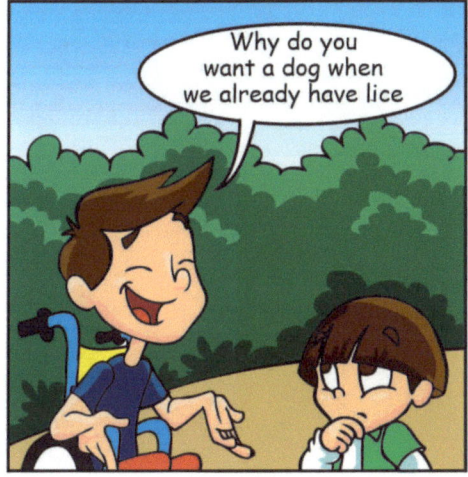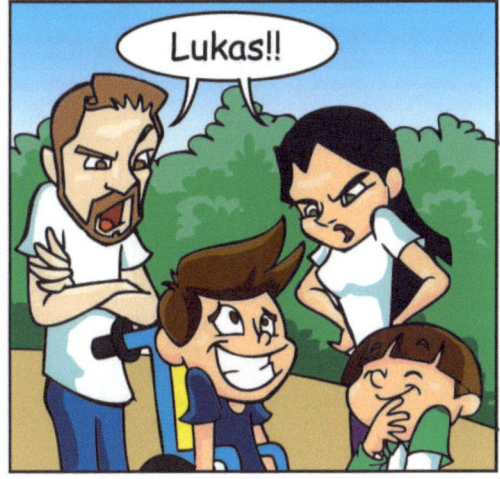

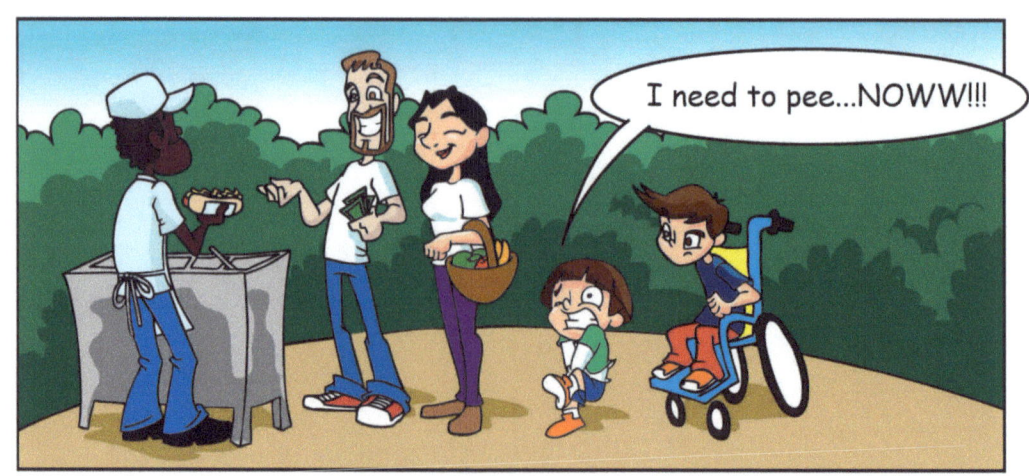
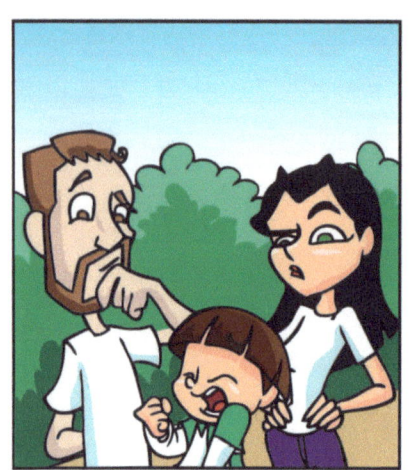
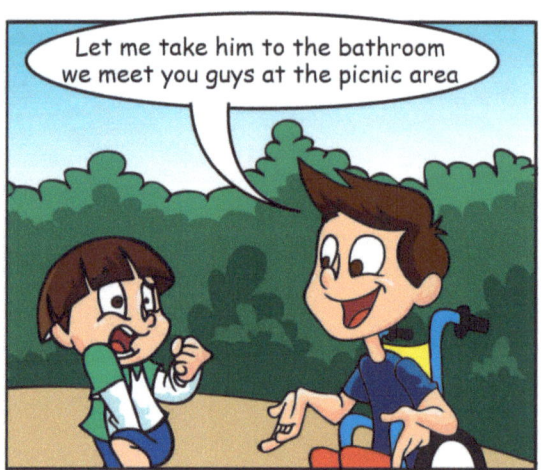
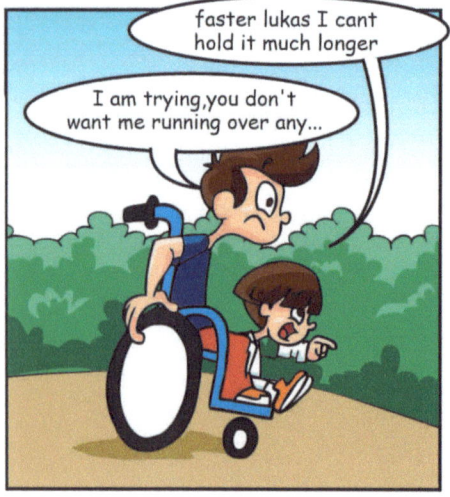
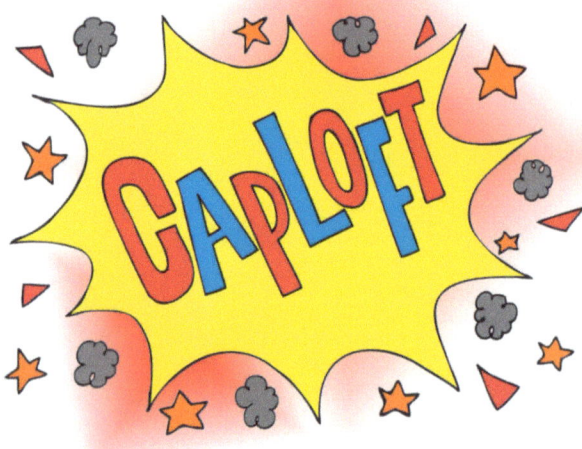

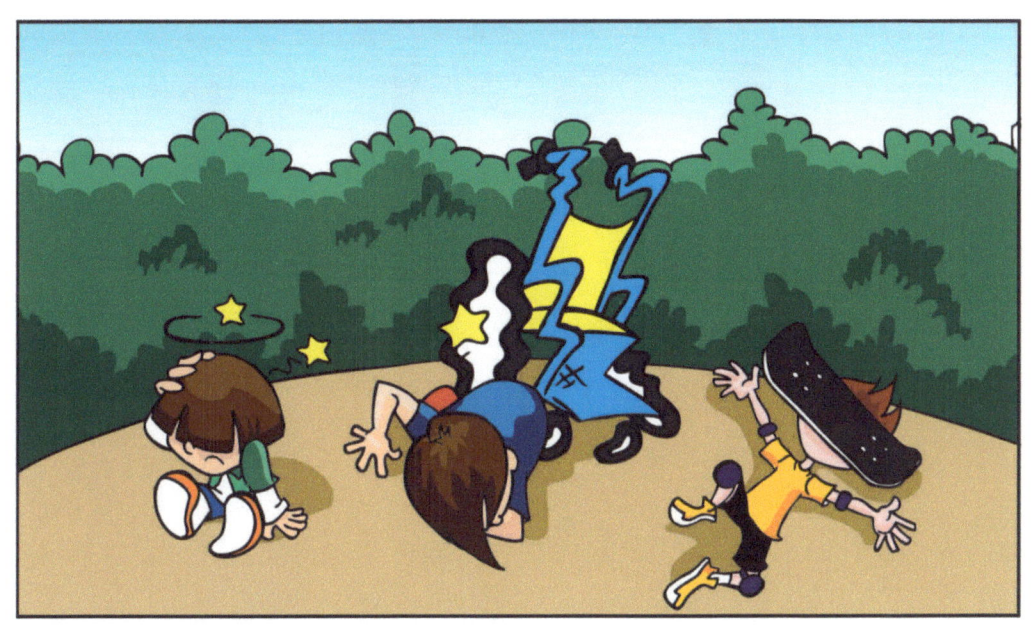
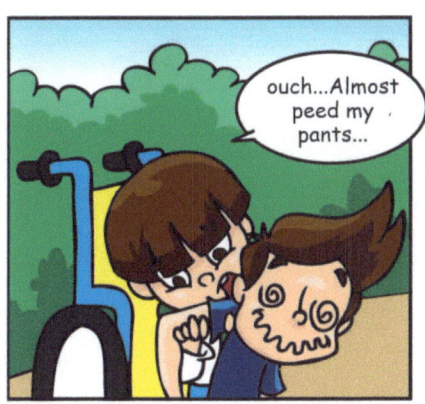
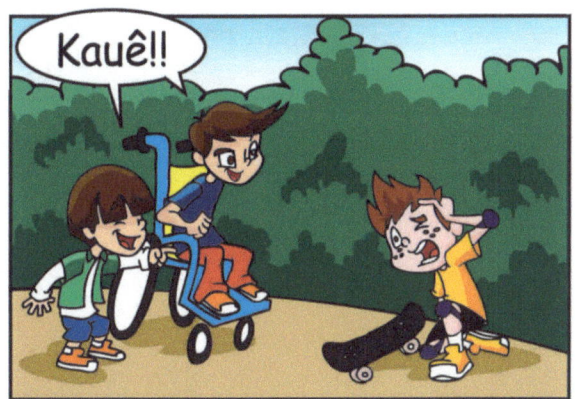
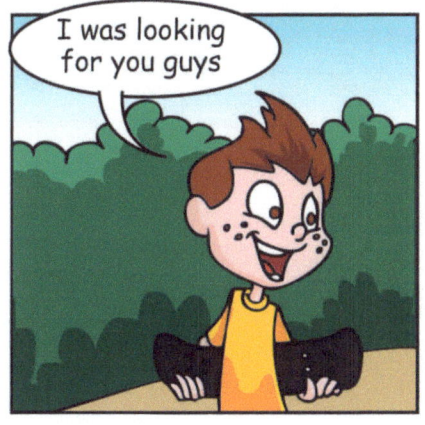
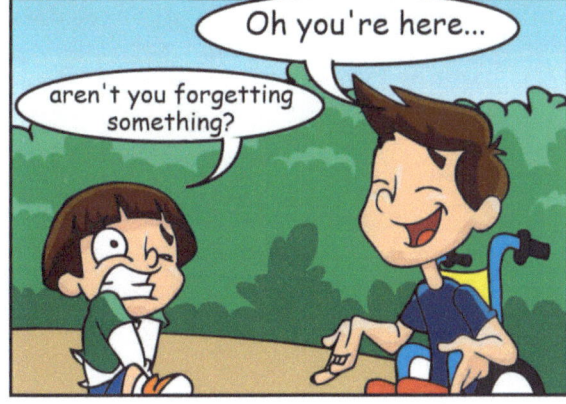

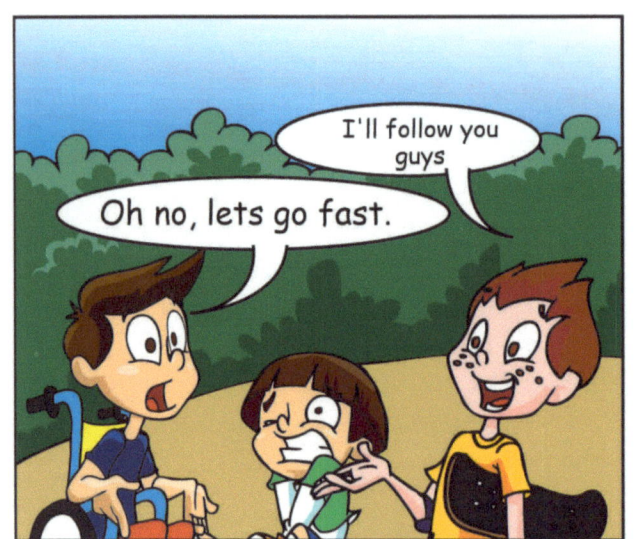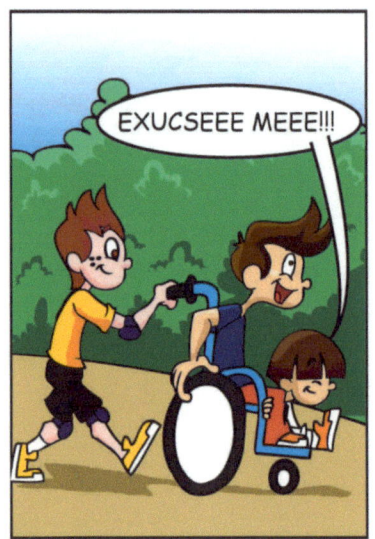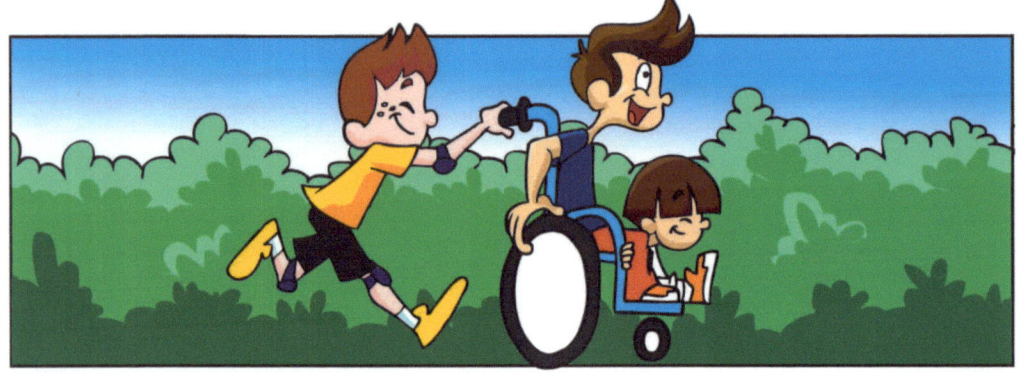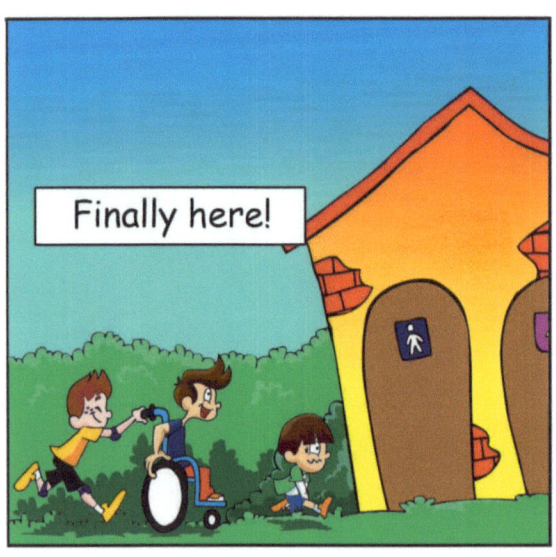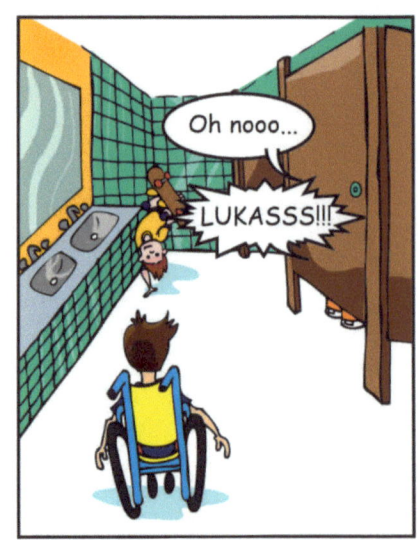

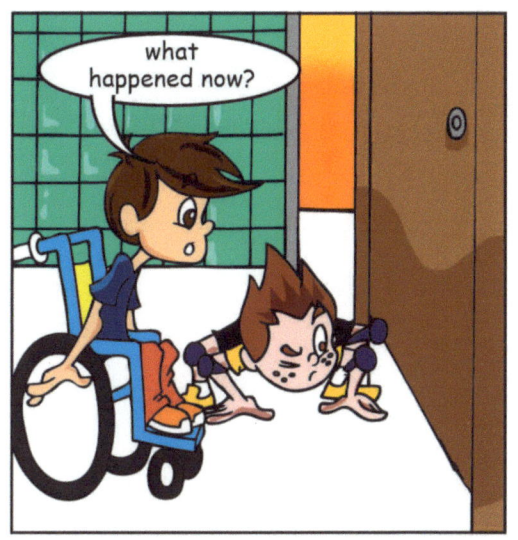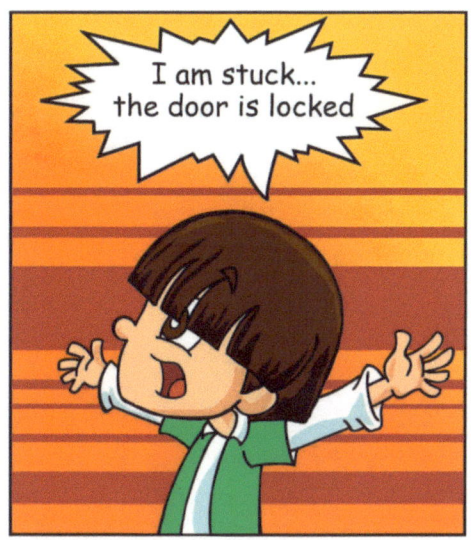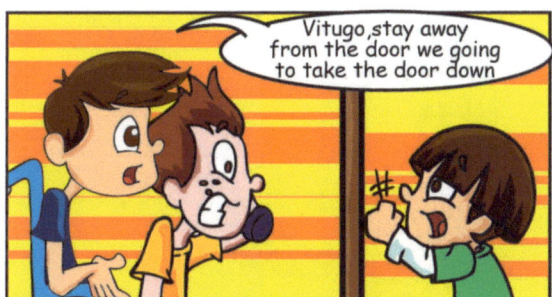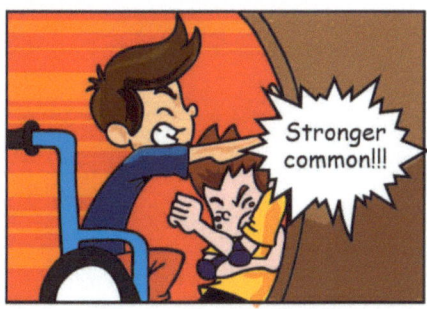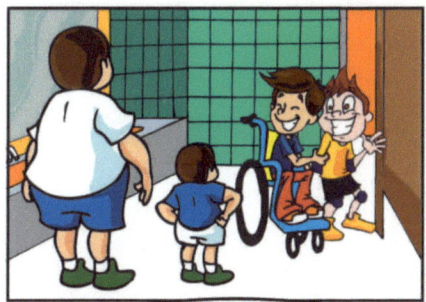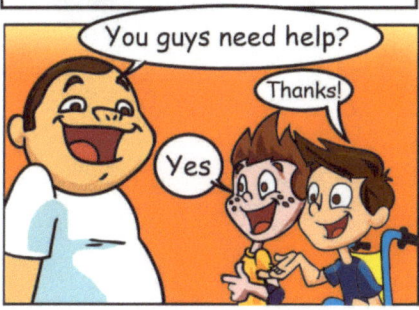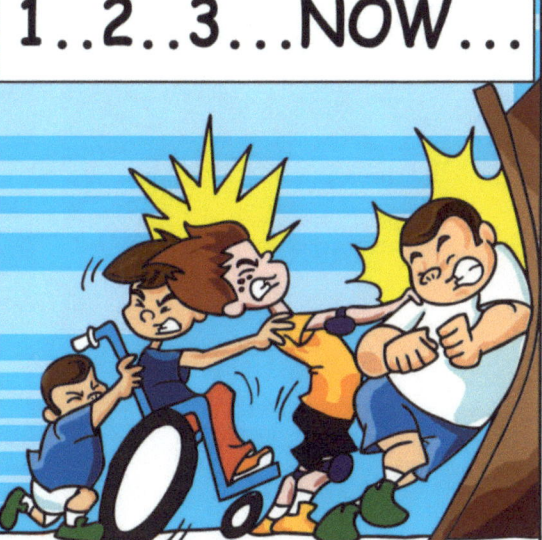

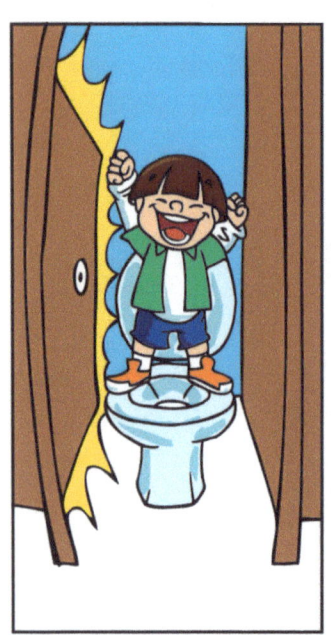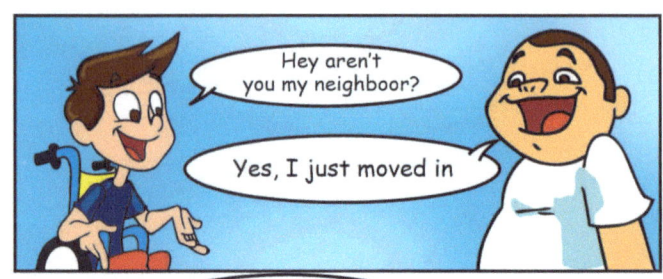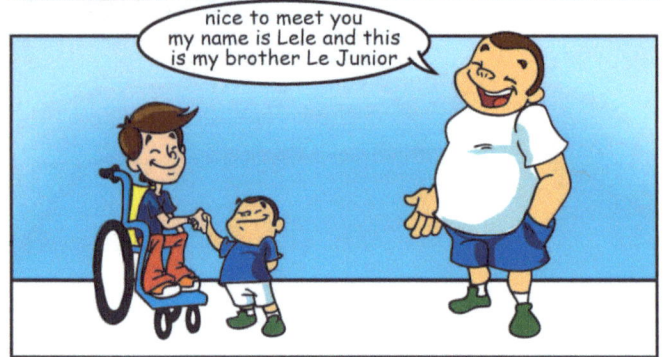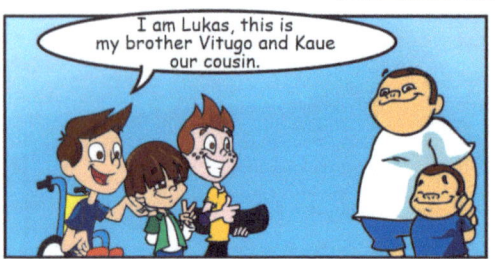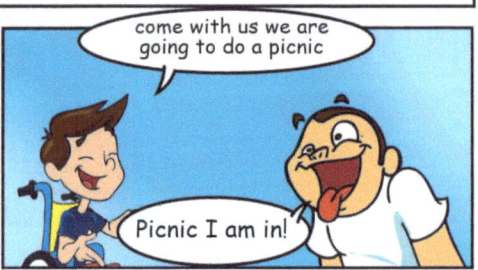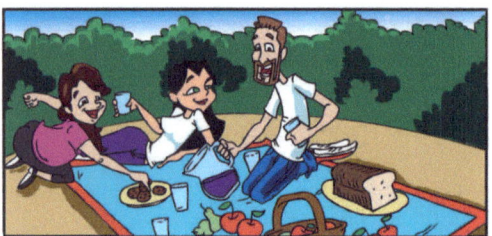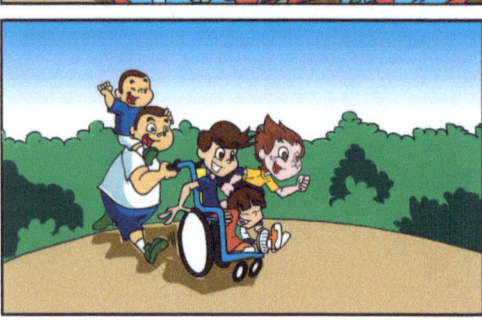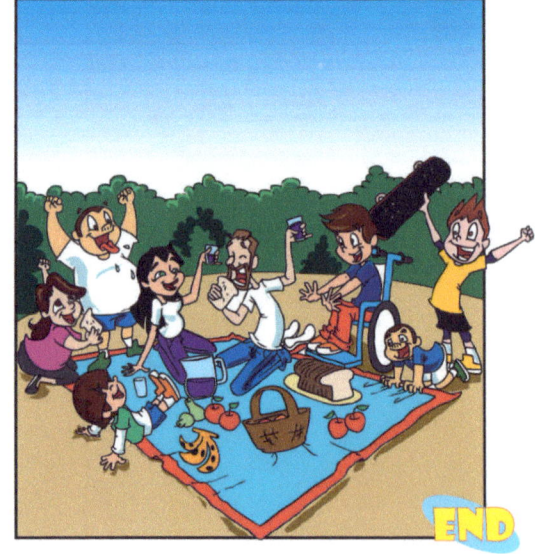

GAME OF THE 7 MISTAKES

"Find the 7 differences in the picture bellow

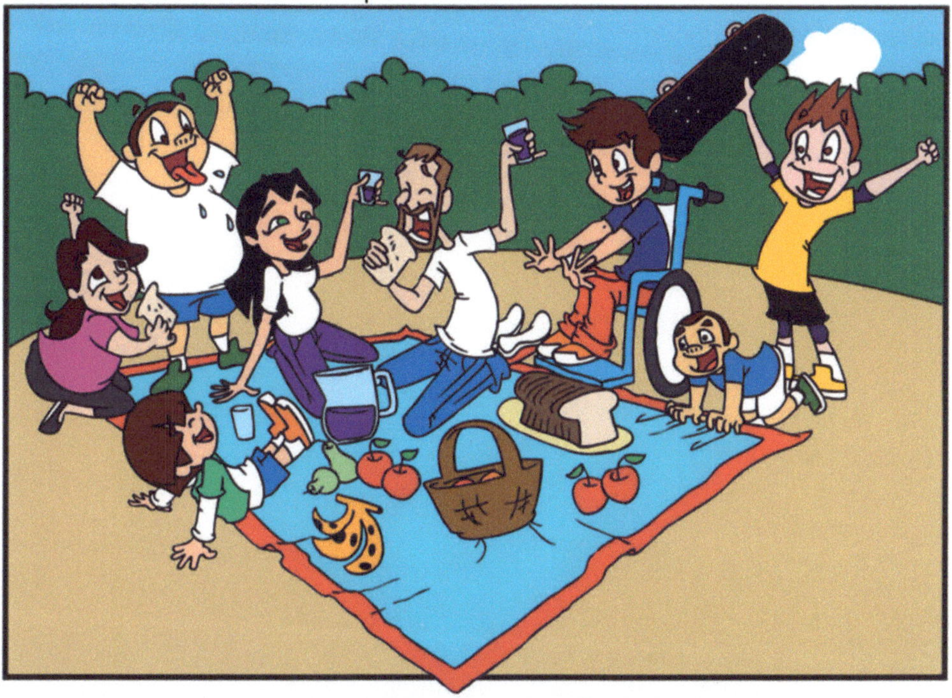

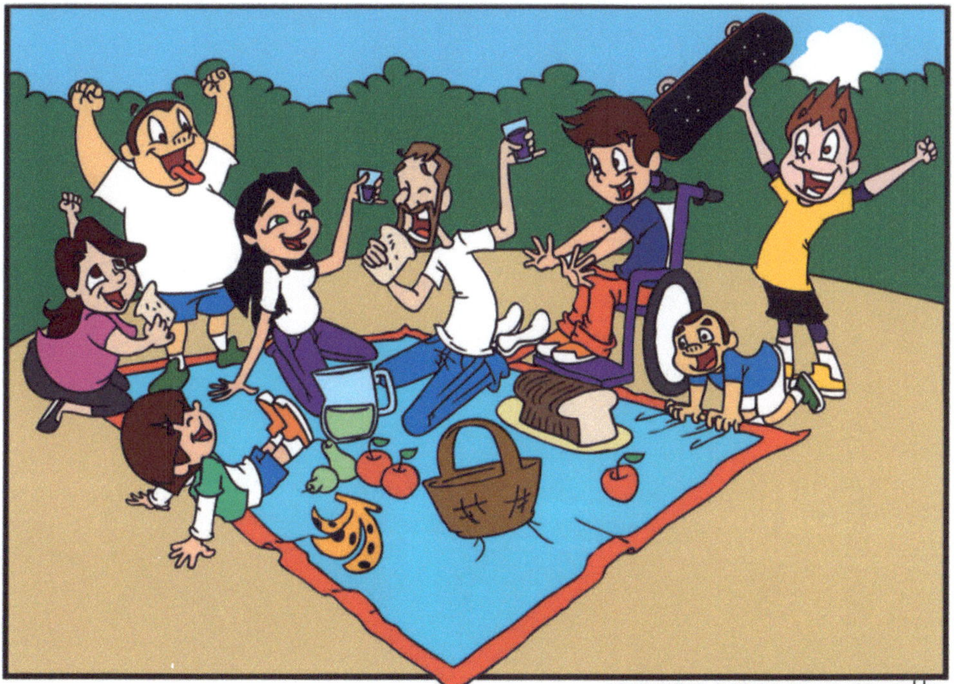

Answers: Lele's mouth/ Cup next to vitugo/ Juice jar/ Fruit Basket/ Carpet next to the bananas/ Apple next to the basket/ Lukas chair

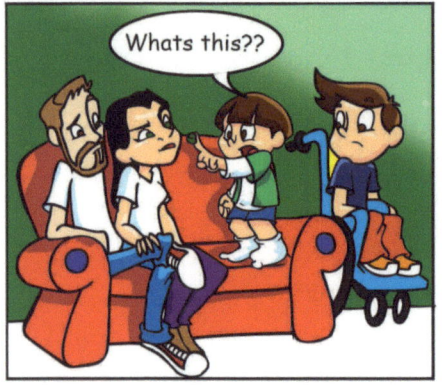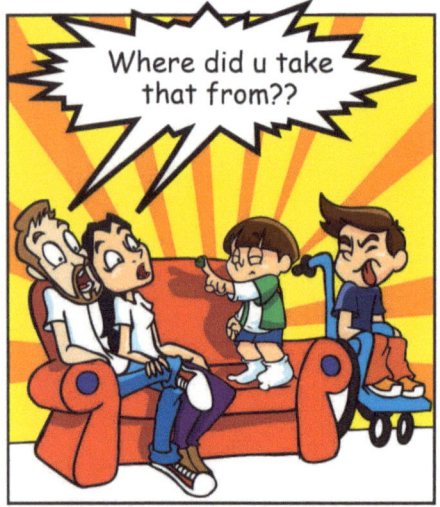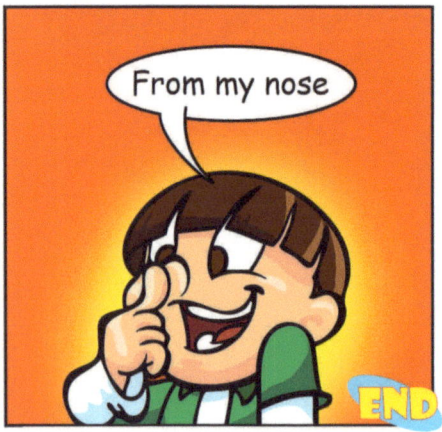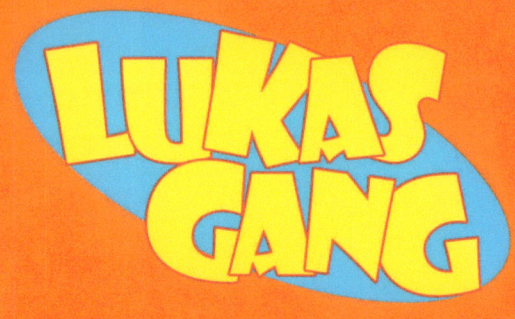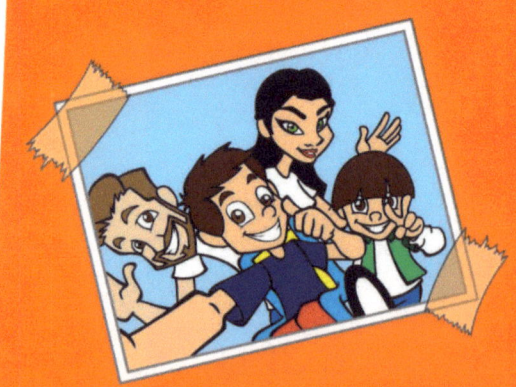

Creation: Fabio Yamashita
Editor: Antonia Yamashita
Illustration: Renan Bressan
Translation: Victor Yamashita
Print: Amazon.com

www.ingramcontent.com/pod-product-compliance
Lightning Source LLC
Chambersburg PA
CBHW041946240526
45473CB00033B/620